The Little Teacup That Talked

EMILIE
BARNES

Illustrated by
MICHAL SPARKS

HARVEST HOUSE PUBLISHERS
EUGENE, OREGON

The Little Teacup That Talked

Text copyright © 2008 by Emilie Barnes
Artwork copyright © 2008 by Michal Sparks
Published by Harvest House Publishers
Eugene, OR 97402
www.harvesthousepublishers.com

ISBN-13: 978-0-7369-2009-4
ISBN-10: 0-7369-2009-9

Design and production by Garborg Design Works, Minneapolis, Minnesota.

The Scripture quotation on page 3 is taken from the International Children's Bible®. Copyright© 1986, 1988, 1999 by Thomas Nelson, Inc. Used by permission. All rights reserved.

Printed in China

08 09 10 11 12 13 14 15 16 / LP / 10 9 8 7 6 5 4 3 2 1

To:

_____

From:

_____

I went down to the potter's house.
I saw him working at the potter's wheel…
He used his hands to shape the pot
the way that he wanted it to be.

THE BOOK OF JEREMIAH

Once upon a time there lived a kindly grandmother and grandfather. Their dear granddaughter was celebrating a special birthday, and they longed to give her just the right gift.
So the couple visited their favorite shop, looking all around for the perfect present.

"Come!" The grandmother suddenly beckoned to the grandfather. "I've found something I want to show you!" She pointed to a most beautiful teacup sitting on the shelf, with a mirror positioned directly behind it.

"Oh, that is indeed the perfect gift!" The grandfather heartily agreed.

Then, much to the couple's surprise, the teacup began to talk.

"I know I look lovely now, but I have not always been this beautiful," it began. "I started out as just an ordinary, gray slab of clay. I had no idea what I was to become. Then a potter picked me up and pressed me into a teacup-shaped mold. He kindly assured me that this was the first step in transforming me from a shapeless lump of clay into an elegant china teacup. But such a change seemed impossible!

"Finally, he removed me from the mold. I was so excited! Was I now a teacup? No, not yet. The potter's hands gently took hold of me, and he explained that the second step was to permanently set my new shape in the kiln. Being in there was like sitting in a sauna or a hot tub or playing outdoors in the hot sunshine.

"As the sweat dripped off of me,
I wondered what this heat had to do with
becoming a teacup. But the potter let
me know it was important, and I knew I
was in the hands of an expert. I'd seen his
work, and his teacups were beautiful.

"At last the kiln cooled down, and the
potter took me out. He placed me on a
counter, and a woman came up to me.
Was I now a teacup? No, not yet.

"The woman took a paintbrush, dipped it in paint, and began to decorate the outside of me with delicate rosebuds. I imagined I looked quite pretty, but I could not see myself. The paintbrush began to tickle.

"'This tickles!' I giggled. 'I know,' the artist smiled, stopping to give me a break. 'How I wish you could see yourself! You look so pretty! Now, let's add a bit more pink.'"

"When she finished painting the rosebuds, the artist dipped a fine-tipped brush in gold paint and began to brush a delicate band of gold all the way around me. Was I now a teacup? No, not yet.

"And then she put me back in the kiln again, where I fanned myself and wondered when on earth I would become a real teacup. It seemed to be taking such a long time! There were so many steps in the process! But the potter and the artist had been so gentle and caring that I trusted them.

"I was taken out of the kiln by a new set of hands and placed in a square room surrounded by soft, white foamy pillows. Where was I now? I began to tumble and roll, not knowing which way was up and which way was down. This must be what it was like to ride a roller coaster! Where would I end up? I was confused, but at the same time I felt safe and protected. Was I now a teacup? No, not yet.

"Suddenly the motion stopped, and a lady picked me up—the same lady who owns this delightful shop. She lovingly set me on this very shelf, and when I looked in the mirror that was placed behind me, I realized at last what I looked like. 'I am beautiful!' I exclaimed with surprise. 'I am now a teacup.'"

As the grandmother held in her hand the precious teacup with the wonderful story, she thought of what she might say to her granddaughter when she presented her with the gift.

She might tell her that just as there will be times of happiness and celebration in her life, there will also be times of sadness and hurt. A close friend might move away. She might struggle with a subject in school. She might lose something special. The grandmother would share with her beloved granddaughter that there would be times of disappointment and heartache as well as times of love and joy.

The grandfather looked at the teacup cradled gently in his wife's hand, and he determined to tell his granddaughter its story. He longed for her to know that the process of becoming beautiful on the inside as well as the outside can take a long time, with many steps. As he looked at the other teacups on the shelf, he noticed that some had minor imperfections—a tiny chip here, a little crack there.

"Did you notice this little chip in the cup?" the grandmother asked, examining a small dent.

"I still think it's perfect for our granddaughter," the grandfather replied. He thought back to all the times in his own life when he felt as though he'd been dropped—when his heart had been broken, when a friend had let him down, when he'd stayed awake late at night with other troubles and worries. He imagined all the chips and cracks in his life and in his wife's life coming together to perfect them, to make them into the man and woman God created them to be. He took his wife's hand.

The shop owner approached the couple. "Is there anything I can help you with?" she asked.

"Please wrap this teacup for us," the grandfather said with a smile. "It's absolutely perfect."